Garden Journal and Planner

Michelle Marsh

New Edition, Updated & Expanded

Copyright © 2014, 2017 by Michelle Marsh. Manufactured in the United States of America. All rights reserved. No part of this book may be reproduced or transmitted in any form or by any means, electronic, mechanical, photocopying, recording, or otherwise, including information storage and retrieval systems, without permission in writing from the author/publisher.

Contact Information:

email: gardenjournal129@gmail.com

Twitter: @mygardenbook

Website: http://gottagarden.com

*Dedicated to my kids,
Sean and Kelly*

A gardener's best tool is the knowledge from previous seasons. — *Andy Tomolonis*

To plant a garden is to believe in tomorrow. — *Audrey Hepburn*

Gardening is a medicine that does not need a prescription. And with no limit on dosage. — *Author Unknown*

 I think this is what hooks me to gardening: it is the closest one can come to being present at creation. — *Phyllis Greer*

I am writing in the garden. To write as one should of a garden, one must write not outside or merely somewhere   near it, but in the garden. — *Frances Hodgson Burnett*

Contents

KNOW YOUR GARDENING ZONES   7

The USDA Plant Hardiness Zone Map   9
Sunset Climate Zone   10
The AHS Plant Heat Zones Map   11

GARDEN JOURNAL   13

Each month contains a list of suggested garden tasks for that month, a page for writing that month's to-do list, and journal writing pages.
What to Put In Your Garden Journal?   13

How to Use the Garden Journal If You Live in the Southern Hemisphere   15
January   16
February   22
March   28
April   34
May   40
June   46
July   52
August   58
September   64
October   70
November   76
December   82

GARDEN PLANNER   89

Grid Pages   91-124
Sketch Book and Photo Album   125-162

Contents cont'd

HANDBOOK OF USEFUL GARDEN FORMS 163

Annual Gardening Calendar 164
Seeding Schedule 166
Planting Schedule 168
Pest Control 170
Winners! 172
Losers! 173
Rainfall Amounts 174
Wish List 175
Suppliers, Orders, & Contact Information 176
Expenses 178
Plant Profiles 180

BONUS!

How to Put This Book in a 3-Ring Binder 185
Link to *FREE BOOK:* "Container Gardening" 190

Know Your Gardening Zones

Know Your Gardening Zones!

For happiness in gardening —

- Know the USDA Plant Hardiness Zone for your ZIP code

- Know the AHS Plant Heat Zone for your ZIP code

Will this plant thrive in my area?

That is the question to ask yourself before planting. One of the main factors to consider is temperature. As a gardener you need to know if the plant will withstand your coldest days of winter and your hottest days of summer. How can you find out? Those average high and low temperatures have been mapped out for the United States and other countries, resulting in two maps that are available as tools to help you know which plants will survive in your garden throughout the year. The two maps are: (1) USDA Plant Hardiness Zone Map (based on average lowest temperatures); and (2) AHS Heat Zone Map (based on average highest temperatures). Both are explained below, and both supply information you need to know as a gardener.

You probably are already familiar with USDA Hardiness Zones and check the USDA Zones on seed packets and plant tags before planting. AHS Heat Zones are newer but of equal importance to gardeners. Increasingly you'll find a set of AHS Zone numbers just after the USDA Zones on seed

The USDA Plant Hardiness Zone Map

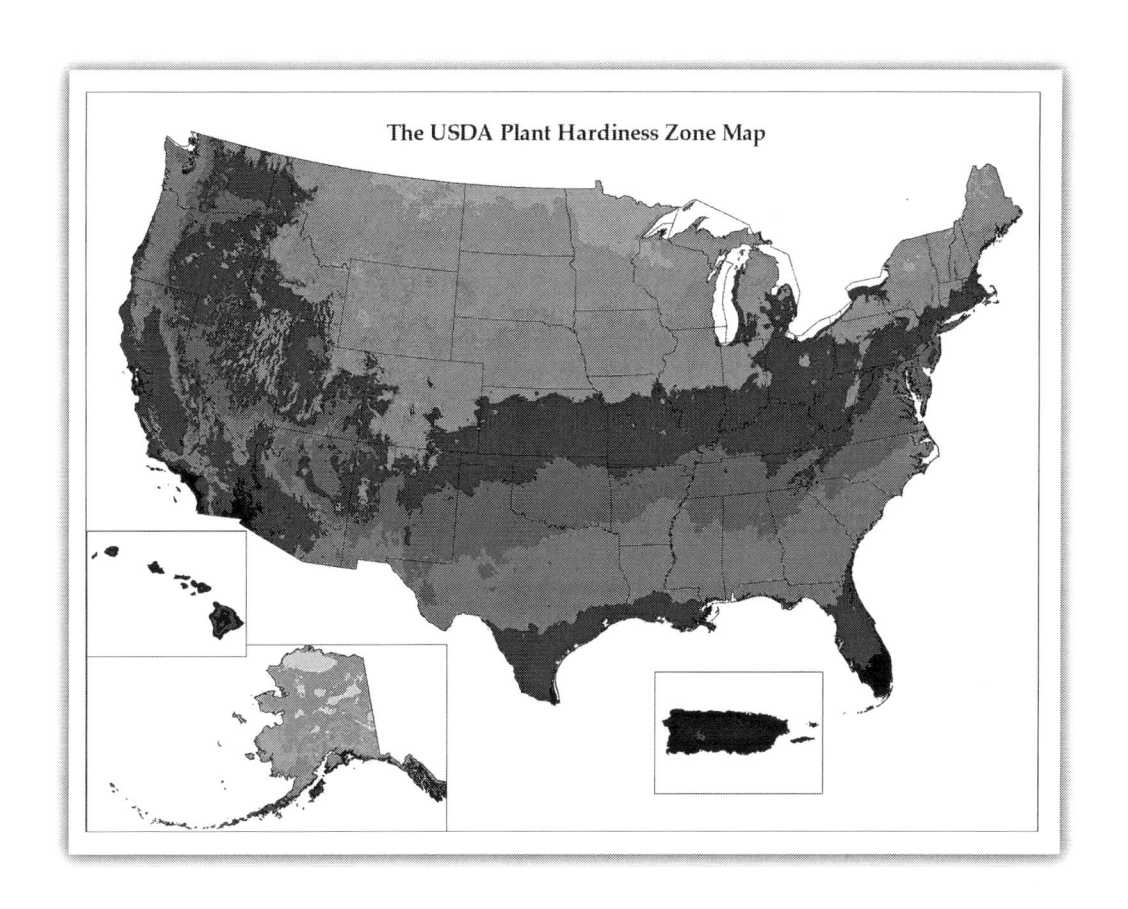

Average Annual Extreme Minimum Temperature 1976-2005		
Temp (F)	Zone	Temp (C)
-60 to -50	1	-51.1 to -45.6
-50 to -40	2	-45.6 to -40
-40 to -30	3	-40 to -34.4
-30 to -20	4	-34.4 to -28.9
-20 to -10	5	-28.9 to -23.3
-10 to 0	6	-23.3 to -17.8
0 to 10	7	-17.8 to -12.2
10 to 20	8	-12.2 to -6.7
20 to 30	9	-6.7 to -1.1
30 to 40	10	-1.1 to 4.4
40 to 50	11	4.4 to 10
50 to 60	12	10 to 15.6
60 to 70	13	15.6 to 21.1

packets and plant tags. Since the release of the AHS Heat Zone Map in 1997, over 15,000 plants have been coded for heat tolerance, with more on the way.

The USDA Plant Hardiness Zone Map

Are You Using the Latest Version? In 1990 the U.S. Department of Agriculture (USDA) published the USDA Plant Hardiness Zone Map as an aid in determining which plants will thrive in the average *lowest* temperatures of a region. It was based on weather data from only a 13-year time period (1974-1986).

In 2012 the USDA released new updated Plant Hardiness Zone Maps for the United States, each state and geographical region, and Puerto Rico.

If you have been using the older map you may find a shift in your zone. The zones in the new map are, in general, about 5°F warmer, although some mountainous regions are cooler. The change is due to data being taken from more weather stations and for a longer period of time. Two new zones were added: Zone 12 and Zone 13. They apply to Hawaii and Puerto Rico.

View the Map on the Internet

The new USDA Plant Hardiness Zone Map was designed to be viewed on the Internet. It is color-coded and has a higher level of resolution than printed versions. Using the Internet version, you can zoom in on very small areas to see exact locations. In addition, the map is interactive for Zip codes. That is, you simply type in your ZIP code to get your hardiness zone. One further advantage is that you can access your state map from the site. To use the interactive version of the map, go to the USDA Plant Hardiness Zone Map website:

http://planthardiness.ars.usda.gov/PHZMWeb/

Plant Hardiness Zones Outside the United States

There are now plant hardiness maps available for most countries. Below are two websites for plant hardiness zones listed by country/continent. Use them to find your plant hardiness zone.

http:www.plantmaps.com

This site has hardiness zone maps for the United States (both national and each state); Canada, Europe (and individual European countries); Australia, China, Japan; South Korea; New Zealand; and South Africa.

www.plantsdb.gr/general-cultivation/hardiness-zones/274=hardiness-zones/274-hardiness-zone-map

This site has a word hardiness zone map as well as hardiness zone maps for: Asia, Africa, North America, Greece, Europe, Central and South America, and Oceania.

It also lists major cities for each or those countries. (AHS Heat Zones are explained beginning on the next page.)

Sunset Climate Zones

If you live in the West you'll find that gardeners, nurseries, and garden centers use *Sunset Climate Zones*, rather than USDA Hardiness Zones. Sunset Zones were developed by *Sunset Magazine* over 40 years ago. They not only factor in lowest winter temperatures, but also summer highs, humidity, length of growing seasons, and rainfall patterns.

If you use Sunset Zones you will still need to know your USDA Zone because USDA Zones are used by the rest of the country, including garden catalogs you order from and books you refer to for plant information.

The AHS Plant Heat Zone Map

The AHS Plant Heat Zone Map is the counterpart to the USDA Hardiness Map. That is, the hardiness map helps gardeners determine if a plant can survive the coldest temperatures of their average winter; the heat zone map helps gardeners determine if a plant can withstand the hottest temperatures of their average summer. Both maps are invaluable to gardeners in deciding what to plant.

What Is the AHS Plant Heat Zone Map? The AHS Map was developed by the American Horticultural Society based on temperature data from the National Climatic Data Center and daily high temperature readings from 4,745 National Weather Service stations throughout the United States from 1974 through 1995. In 1997 the AHS produced a national heat zone map that represented their findings.

The map is divided into 12 zones based on the number of "heat days" in each zone; that is the average number of days the zone experiences temperatures above 86°F (30° C). Zone 1, for example, has fewer than one "heat day" per year (northernmost zone). Zone 12 has over 210 "heat days" per year (parts of Florida, Texas, and Hawaii). Why 86 °F (30°C)? Because that is the temperature at which many plants begin to experience protein damage.

How "Heat Days" Affect Plants

Symptoms of plant heat distress include dropping leaves, fading in color or turning pale blue-green, reducing fruit development, and in some cases, dying. Symptoms may appear suddenly or a plant may linger for years. Even if a heat stressed plan does not die, it is left more vulnerable to disease and insect attack

How to Find Your AHS Heat Zone

The AHS Heat Zone Map is color-coded, as is the new USDA Plant Hardiness Map. It was developed by the same group that worked on the USDA hardiness map.

You can view the AHS Heat Zone Map for the United States on the AHS website: **http://ahsgardening.org/gardening-resources/gardening-maps/heat-zone-map**

The heat zone map on the AHS website is not interactive. That is, you cannot type in your ZIP code to find your AHS heat Zone. It is easy to see your approximate location on the map, however, and to check your heat index using the color-colded map key. State counties are outlined on the map, and AHS offers a 2' x 3' printed version of the map on its website.

An easy-to-use black/white version of the AHS Heat Zone Map labels *each state* with its heat zone number, rather than using color coding . It may be found at:

http://thudscave.com/petroglyphs/pdf/us_heatzones.pdf

If You Live Outside the United States

The AHS Plant Heat-Zone Map is relatively new. To date, heat zone maps are available for Australia and Mexico These are listed below. However, there is a site where you can find the heat zone of a city nearest you. Go to:

    http://www.plantsdb.gr/en/general-cultivation/hardiness-zones/274-hardiness-zones-map

Australia Heat Zone Map
    https://www.diggers.com.au/shop/ordering-information/climate-maps/

Mexico Heat Zone Map
    http://www.redalyc.org/html/609/60911226/index.html\

How to Use Plant Heat Zone Labels

Heat zone labels for plants are appearing ever more frequently in garden catalogs and plant labels, and more plants are continually being assigned heat zones. The heat zone numbers are listed right after the USDA hardiness numbers.

AHS gives this example: The cold-tolerant English wallflower is listed as Zones 5-8, 6-1. The first two numbers are the USDA hardiness zone.. The last two numbers are the AHS heat zone. They mean that the English wallflower will probably not survive a winter colder than USDA Zone 5, and it will not withstand summer heat higher than AHS Heat Zone 6. (It will not survive in Zone 7, for example). Notice that for USDA zones the lowest number (coldest temperature) is listed first. For AHS zones the highest number (hottest temperature) is listed first.

Advantages and Drawbacks of the AHS Map

A big advantage of the AHS Map over the USDA Map is that it assigns zones for annual plants as well as perennials. The AHS Map Zones apply to annual flowers, garden vegetables, herbs, and field crops, as well as to perennials.

Like the USDA Map, the AHS Map should only be used as a guide. It is based on temperature only and does not take into account unusual weather patterns, humidity, or variance in nighttime temperatures. Most important, it assumes that *all plants are getting adequate waier.* AHS advises: "The accuracy of the zone coding can be substantially distorted by a lack of water, even for a brief period in the life of the plant."

Why You Should Know Your Plant Hardiness & Heat Zones

Both too much cold and too much heat are detrimental to garden plants. Knowing your hardiness and heat zones arms you with two tools to help determine which plants will best thrive in your garden

The USDA Plant Hardiness Map, Sunset Map, and AHS Heat Map are useful tools .for your gardening toolbox, designed to help ensure your gardening success. Consult them as needed whenever you're deciding which plants to choose for your garden.

Garden Journal

This journal provides an easy, convenient way to track your garden — to note your gardening activities, observations, and reflections; to record your plans.

Each month of the Journal contains:

- ☐ A list of suggested garden tasks for that month

- ☐ A page to write a to-do list for that month

- ☐ Journal pages to record what you did and when; the weather; your observations and impressions; what worked and what didn't; your thoughts and reflections; notes for next year's garden; a wish list of garden tools and supplies — and more!

What to Put In Your Garden Journal?

- What seeds you bought and where you bought them
- How you amended the soil
- Planting dates and where you planted what
- Transplanting dates
- What blooms when? What is the length of the plant's blooming cycle?
- Rate plants' general performance. Which deserve a 10? Which aren't worth it?
- What works? Evaluate your fertilizers, soil amendments, insecticides, fungicides
- Rainfall: When did it rain? Amount? Where did it pool in your garden?
- Harvesting dates and crop yields
- Weather conditions with dates. First and last frost dates
- Activities: E.g., till, water, fertilize, plant, mulch, weed, prune
- Plant/seed buying: What bought? Where? When? How many? Plant size? Cost?
- Wish List: Plants, garden accents, equipment, books, techniques you'd like to try
- Garden pests you encountered and how you dealt with them
- Photos and sketches of your plants and garden beds; garden plans and designs; pictures and magazine articles of dream gardens; plant tags
- Expenses, receipts, and contacts for your garden suppliers.

Websites With Monthly Gardening Tips

WEEKEND GARDENER:
http://www.weekendgardener.net/do-list.htm

ROYAL HORTICULTURAL SOCIETY:
https://www.rhs.org.uk/ advice/in-month/

How to Use This Garden Journal If You Live in the Southern Hemisphere

You'll notice that at the end of each month suggestions are given on what to do in the garden that month. Those suggestions are based on that month's season in the northern hemisphere. But the seasons are reversed in the northern and southern hemispheres. In the northern hemisphere, for example, the winter months are December, January, and February. In the southern hemisphere the winter months are June, July, and August.

If you live in the southern hemisphere how can you adapt the journal so that the gardening suggestions are appropriate for the month? It's an easy fix. Just cross out the names of the months in the journal section and replace them with your corresponding months in the southern hemisphere.

CHANGE	to	THIS
January		July
February		August
March		September
April		October
May		November
June		December
July		January
August		February
September		March
October		April
November		May
December		June

January

What to Do In the Garden

- ☐ **Plan this year's garden.** Before you put in your order for spring seeds, make a scale drawing of your plans for your garden and planting beds. Show their location and size. Check your leftover seeds and throw away any that are too old.

- ☐ **Browse through seed catalogs.** Make a list of the seeds you want. Many varieties sell out early, so order your seeds now to avoid substitutions. Order seed-starting materials, as well.

- ☐ **Check your garden tools.** Organize, clean, oil, and sharpen them, as needed. Check power tools to see if they need a tune-up, oil change, new air filter, etc. Consider painting wooden tool handles a bright color to preserve the wood and make them easy to spot.

- ☐ **Check bulbs you have stored.** Discard any that are moldy, soft, discolored, or rotting. Repack those that are too damp. Move any that have sprouted to a cooler location.

- ☐ **Start pruning** dormant fruit trees, grapes, and shrubs.

- ☐ **Recycle** your Christmas tree and holiday plants. Use the branches as a mulch and to provide cover for birds. Move live Christmas trees outside. Put them in partial shade a week before planting.

For warmer regions:

- ☐ **Test your soil's pH.** Then apply lime, sulfur, and fertilizer as needed.

- ☐ **Spread and plow under manure** and compost if you did not do so in the fall.

- ☐ **Prepare planting beds and seed boxes.** Mix in organic materials. Plant hardy vegetables, cool-season crops and annuals, bulbs that have been refrigerated (cover with mulch), and trees and shrubs. (Water until they are established.)

- ☐ **Plant hardy vegetables,** cool-season crops, bulbs that have been refrigerated (cover with mulch), and trees and shrubs. (Water until they are established.

- ☐ **Sow seeds** of annual flowers wherever you want flowers for cutting or as a background for other plants. Some good choices are: delphiniums, snapdragons, and larkspur.

- ☐ **Apply dormant oil spray** to fruit trees whose buds have not opened.

For colder regions:

- ☐ **Shake or brush off snow** from branches weighed down without support. Remove damaged branches.

- ☐ *Thicken mulch* over emerging bulbs that were pushed out of the ground by alternate freezing and thawing.

- ☐ **Limit traffic** over your frozen lawn.

January To-Do List

Week 1

Week 2

Week 3

Week 4

January Journal

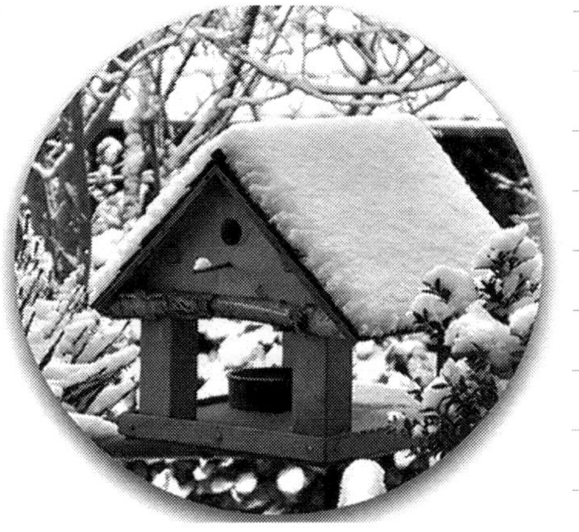

January Journal (cont'd)

February

What to Do In the Garden

- ☐ **Continue to plan your garden.** Order seeds and seed-starting supplies if you have not yet done so. Buy compost, if needed.

- ☐ **Start seeds indoors for transplanting.** They should be started no sooner than 6-8 weeks before your last frost date. (If you start earlier, transplants are likely to be too leggy.) Grow your seedlings on a window sill with a southern exposure or under lights. They will need 10-16 hours of light per day.

- ☐ **Prune dormant fruit trees** before new buds open. Prune evergreens that have needles.

- ☐ **Fertilize established fruit trees** after the last frost.

- ☐ **When snow melts** and you can see the ground, plant seeds of perennials, such as delphiniums, lupines, and hollyhocks.

- ☐ **Cover the seeds lightly** with compost.

- ☐ **When the soil is workable,** dig in manure or compost.

- ☐ **Plant garlic and onions.**

- ☐ **When the first crocus opens,** set out transplants of cool-season vegetables. Cover them when nights are cold

For warmer regions:

- ☐ **Harvest winter crops** before they bolt.

- ☐ **Plant dahlia bulbs** and begonia tubers, asparagus and strawberries

- ☐ **Sow seeds** of radishes, lettuce and other greens. Repeat sowing every two weeks for a continuous harvest.

- ☐ **When the soil is warm,** plant potatoes.

- ☐ **Prune roses and fruit trees.** Spray fruit trees if you've had trouble with leaf or fruit diseases. Wait to prune fruit trees until after they bloom.

- ☐ **Dig in compost** and cover crops.

- ☐ **Start seeds inside under lights** for transplanting: tomatoes, peppers, eggplant, cauliflower, petunias, begonias, geraniums.

- ☐ **In Zone 10, plant:** (1) cucumber and corn seeds; (2) hot-pepper transplants; (3) fast-growing beets, radishes, and carrots; (4) "Southern" vegetables, such as okra and sweet potatoes.

For colder regions:

- ☐ **Prune ornamentals,** fruit trees, and bushes. Hard-prune holly bushes.

- ☐ **Push down perennials** that may have heaved after a frost followed by thawing.

- ☐ **Water evergreens if needed.**

- ☐ **Replace mulch.**

February To-Do List

Week 1

Week 2

Week 3

Week 4

February Journal

February Journal (cont'd)

March

What to Do In the Garden

- ☐ **Plant cold-hardy annuals,** such as pansies and violas.

- ☐ **Plant potatoes** when the grass begins to green.

- ☐ **Plant grapes** when the soil is workable. (In the South, plant them in the fall.)

- ☐ **As temperatures warm,** begin to remove mulch.

- ☐ **Transplant** ornamental trees, roses, and shrubs before leaf buds open.

- ☐ **Prune bush roses** before the new growth begins.

- ☐ **Don't walk on wet soil** or work in garden beds until the ground starts to dry after the spring thaw.

- ☐ **Fertilize** shrubs and perennials.

- ☐ **Sow seeds** of half-hardy annuals, such as phlox, ageratum, French marigold, and snapdragon, indoors under lights or on a windowsill.

- ☐ **Divide perennials.**

- ☐ **Prune shrubs,** including winter- and spring- flowering shrubs.

- ☐ **Provide support** for "climbers."

- ☐ **For evergreens:** remove weak or damaged growth.

- ☐ **Take cuttings** of pelargonium and fuchsia to have flowering plants by summer.

For warmer regions:

- ☐ **A dormant oil spray** can be used on fruit trees in the upper South.

- ☐ **Plant summer vegetables** and summer flower bulbs.

For colder regions:

- ☐ **Plant strawberries** and cool-weather vegetable transplants.

- ☐ **Plant lettuce**, but cover when frost is forecast.

- ☐ **Add lime to the soil** where you plan to plant tomatoes (next month).

- ☐ **Start tomato seeds indoors,** as well as other warm-season vegetables and herbs that can be transplanted. Seeds for cool-season crops can be planted outdoors now.

March To-Do List

Week 1

Week 2

Week 3

Week 4

March Journal

March Journal (cont'd)

April

What to Do In the Garden

- ☐ **Fill in extra space in your garden** with warm-season annuals.

- ☐ **Plant trees.** However, try to fill in the planting hole with original soil. Adding organic matter may discourage roots from sprouting beyond the planting hole.

- ☐ **Remove mulch and debris.**

- ☐ **Prepare planting beds** by weeding and digging in compost.

- ☐ **Sow seeds** of herbs, vegetables, and quick-flowering annuals.

- ☐ **Plant hyacinths and tulips** until the end of the month.

- ☐ **Plant root vegetables.** Beans, broccoli, cabbage, kale, kohlrabi, lettuce, and peas may still be grown from seed.

- ☐ **Harden off seedlings.** Move seeds sown indoors to a cold frame or sheltered porch a week or so before moving them outside.

- ☐ **Feed established container plants.**

For warmer regions:

- ☐ **Transplant perennials** grown in containers.

- ☐ **Sow seeds of lettuce and greens** every two weeks to ensure a continuing harvest.

- ☐ **Continue sowing melons,** squash, and beans, as well as Southern vegetables.

- ☐ **Except in the upper regions of the South, plant seedlings** of tomatoes, peppers, and eggplant.

- ☐ **Replace mulch** around flowering shrubs.

- ☐ **Plant heat-loving herbs,** such as basil.

- ☐ **Prune flowering shrubs** when they have finished flowering.

- ☐ **When the overnight temperatures** remain above 50°F, move over-wintered tropical plants outdoors.

- ☐ **Plant seedlings** of heat-loving flowering summer annuals, such as zinnias.

For colder regions:

- ☐ **Rake garden beds** to remove dead or decaying matter before plants start growing.

- ☐ **Turn over the soil** in your beds of annual vegetables. Rake away debris that is covering perennial vegetables, such as asparagus and rhubarb.

- ☐ **By the end of the month,** sow seeds of lettuce and snow peas.

- ☐ **Start seeds indoors** of summer vegetables, such as tomatoes, either in a south-facing window or under lights.

April To-Do List

Week 1

Week 2

Week 3

Week 4

April Journal

April Journal (cont'd)

May

What to Do In the Garden

- ☐ **Plant seeds** or transplant seedlings of summer annual flowers.
- ☐ **Plant summer bulbs,** such as canna lilies and dahlias.
- ☐ **Plant asparagus roots,** potato and sweet potato tubers, and strawberry plants.
- ☐ **Plant seeds or seedlings** of perennial herbs such as lemon balm, anise, hyssop, and bee balm.
- ☐ **In the middle of the month,** plant seeds of cool-weather crops to extend harvests.
- ☐ **Transplant seedlings** of warm-weather vegetables and herbs.
- ☐ **Clear rose beds of debris.**
- ☐ **Deadhead and fertilize** re-blooming roses.
- ☐ **Deadhead flowering shrubs** when their blossoms fade. Prune if needed.
- ☐ **Deadhead spring-flowering bulbs,** but allow their foliage to yellow.
- ☐ **Deadhead early-blooming flowers** such as pansies and primroses.
- ☐ **Pinch back mums** after they are 6" to 8" tall to maintain their compact form.
- ☐ **Divide perennials;** stake tall perennials.
- ☐ **Transplant** small trees and shrubs.
- ☐ **Apply mulches.**
- ☐ **Take measures to control insect pests;** e.g., use slug-and-snail bait.
- ☐ **Plant hanging baskets.**
- ☐ **Remove tent-caterpillar nests** and soak the tents in a jar of rubbing alcohol.

For warmer regions:

- ☐ **Sow warm-weather vegetable seeds.**
- ☐ **Replace** cool-season annual flowers with heat-loving annuals.
- ☐ **Finish planting** new citrus trees and berry bushes for a late harvest.
- ☐ **Prune flowering trees and shrubs** when they finish blooming.
- ☐ **Clean up** drooping or ragged fronds on palm trees.
- ☐ **Prune and fertilize roses.** Check for mildew and black spot diseases and water early in the day to control them.
- ☐ **Plant container-grown trees,** shrubs, perennial herbs and ground covers in all but the hottest regions of the South.

For colder regions:

- ☐ **Harvest cool-weather crops** and re-seed for continuing harvests.
- ☐ **Plant warm-weather melon seeds.**
- ☐ **Until the end of the month,** plant seeds of annual flowers and transplant annual seedlings.
- ☐ **Prune and fertilize roses** after they bloom.
- ☐ **Plant summer bulbs.**
- ☐ **Plant/transplant** trees and shrubs.

May To-Do List

Week 1

Week 2

Week 3

Week 4

May Journal

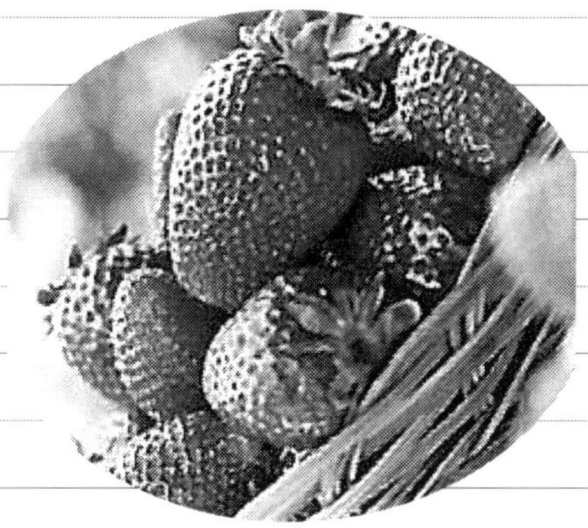

May Journal (cont'd)

JUNE
What to Do In the Garden

- ☐ **Last chance** for planting warm-season vegetables.
- ☐ **Keep newly planted trees** and shrubs well-watered.
- ☐ **Check your roses** for pests and diseases. Treat as needed.
- ☐ **Sow seeds for biennials,** such as hollyhocks, for blooms next year.
- ☐ **Divide spring flowering irises** and Oriental poppies after they bloom.
- ☐ **Deadhead spring-flowering shrubs** and prune them after they bloom.
- ☐ **Mulch** broad-leaf evergreens with an acidic mulch.
- ☐ **Plant trees,** shrubs, ground covers and vines before summer sets in.
- ☐ **Protect fruit from insect pests.** Use an organic spray. Bag some fruit in plastic bags with room for growth.
- ☐ **Use insecticidal soap** to control aphids **and use slug bait for slugs.**
- ☐ **Plant seedlings** of heat loving vegetables such as eggplant, peppers, summer squash, and cauliflower.
- ☐ **Sow seeds** of beans, cucumbers, spinach, parsnips, radishes, squash, and pumpkins.
- ☐ **Plant seedlings or seeds** of cool-weather crops: beets, broccoli, Brussels sprouts, cabbage, carrots, onions, chicory, and kohlrabi.
- ☐ **Plant tender herbs,** such as cilantro and coriander, as well as oregano, parsley, sage, and thyme.
- ☐ **Replace cool-season flowers and crops,** such as spinach that has bolted. Pinch off tomato suckers and keep tomatoes staked.
- ☐ **Protect berries** with nets or row covers.
- ☐ **Clear up** any fallen fruit from fruit trees.

For warmer regions:
- ☐ **Replace cool-season crops** with warm-season crops, e.g., beans, corn, pumpkins, and squash.
- ☐ **Plant summer-flowering bulbs** and seedlings of summer vegetables and late-summer flowering annuals.
- ☐ **Plant** fall-blooming perennials.
- ☐ **Last chance** to plant heat-loving summer-flower bulbs.
- ☐ **Mulch** trees and shrubs.
- ☐ **Plant annuals,** such as impatiens, hosta, and marigolds.

For colder regions:
- ☐ **Prune** spring-flowering trees and shrubs after they finish flowering. Wait until the end of the month to mulch vegetables
- ☐ **Stake** or cage tomato plants; stake other tall-growing vegetables.
- ☐ **Harden transplants** of summer vegetables before replanting. Protect seedlings from wind with thin-wood windbreaks.
- ☐ **Wait until the end of the month** to mulch vegetables.

June To-Do List

Week 1

Week 2

Week 3

Week 4

June Journal

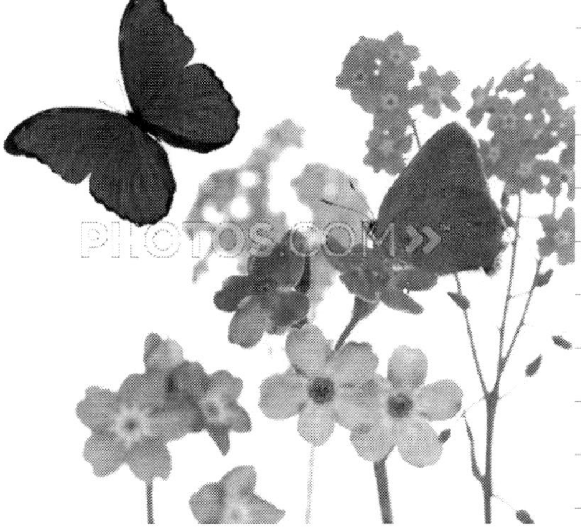
PHOTOS.COM

June Journal (cont'd)

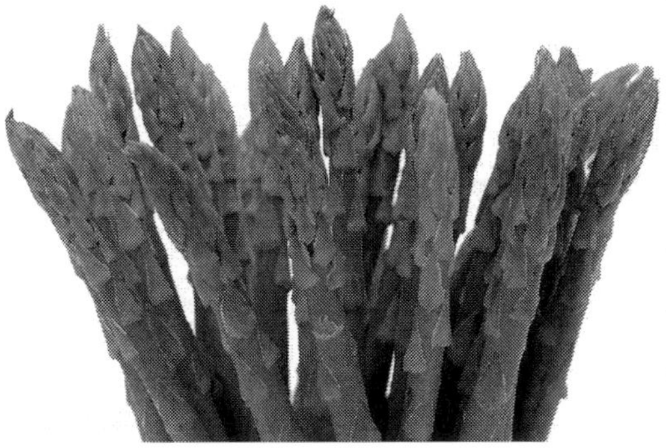

July

What to Do In the Garden

- ☐ **Slow down** and give you and your plants a rest from the heat.
- ☐ **Don't neglect weeding.** Do it regularly.
- ☐ **Give plants a mid-season feeding** or side dressing.
- ☐ **Replace mulch** as needed.
- ☐ **Continue deadheading** flowering ornamentals.
- ☐ **Harvest vegetables daily.**
- ☐ **Re-seed** beans and lettuce.
- ☐ **Prune trees and shrubs** when their blossoms fade.
- ☐ **Trim boxwood and hedges** grown as shaped specimens.
- ☐ **Don't fertilize** if the weather turns dry or there is a drought.
- ☐ **Keep potted plants watered.**
- ☐ **Plant vegetable seed**s for the fall. Check vegetable packets and time your planting so as to harvest before the first frost.
- ☐ **If your fruit trees are carrying a huge crop**, reduce the number of fruits to avoid broken branches and too-small fruit.
- ☐ **After strawberries have fruited,** cut off most of the old leaves.
- ☐ **Prune berry bushes** after the fruit has been picked.
- ☐ **Plant bulbs.**
- ☐ *Take cuttings of shrubs.* Pot them and cover with a plastic bag.
- ☐ **Propagate vines** by layering (pinning part of the stem into the soil.) Examples include wisteria, clematis, and honeysuckle.

For warmer regions:

- ☐ **Harvest summer vegetables.**
- ☐ **In the warmer regions of the South** you can now plant container-grown citrus trees and tropical fruit plants.
- ☐ **Provide a deep-watering** for your plants every 10-14 days.
- ☐ **Remove spent flowers** on crepe myrtle, but don't prune. Also don't prune azaleas

For colder regions:

- ☐ **Weed** and then apply mulch.
- ☐ **Divide irises** and cut back to six inches.
- ☐ **Sow cool-weather vegetable seeds.**
- ☐ **Deadhead perennials.** Prune tall perennials and annual flowers.
- ☐ **Harvest onions** when their tops begin to fall over. Harvest garlic when the leaves start to turn brown.

July To-Do List

Week 1

Week 2

Week 3

Week 4

July Journal

July Journal (cont'd)

August

What to Do In the Garden

- ☐ **Sow seeds** of cool-season vegetables and **annuals.**
- ☐ **Divide irises.**
- ☐ **Harvest vegetables** continually to maintain productivity.
- ☐ **Prune summer-flowering shrubs** after they have finished blooming.
- ☐ **Plant garlic** for spring harvests.
- ☐ **Plan and plant a fall garden** with crops that will mature before the first frost.
- ☐ **Add compost** before planting and moisten the soil. After planting, keep the soil cool with a light covering of straw. Protect seedlings with shade cloth or plant them where they will get shade from taller plants.
- ☐ **Or, start fall-garden seeds indoors** under lights and transplant after 4 to 6 weeks.
- ☐ **Cover root crops with mulch** so you'll be able to harvest them in winter.
- ☐ **Stop fertilizing roses.** Stop dead heading repeat-blooming roses.

For warmer regions:

- ☐ **Shrubs and trees that are setting buds** for next year's blooms need a weekly deep watering. Plants with winter berries also benefit from consistent watering.
- ☐ **Cut back everblooming roses** and prune dead stems. Fertilize and add mulch.
- ☐ **In upper regions of the South** plant vegetables for fall: e.g., lettuce, spinach, turnips, beets. Plant transplants of collards, broccoli, and cauliflower.
- ☐ **Divide spring-flowering perennials,** such as poppies and irises.
- ☐ **In Florida and coastal areas** transplant tomatoes, peppers, and eggplant. Sow seeds of squash, beans, and cucumbers.
- ☐ **Sow wildflowers;** e.g., bluebonnets, coreopsis, and Indian paintbrush.

For colder regions:

- ☐ **Keep your plants well-watered.** Water deeply, slowly, and less often.
- ☐ **Prune back or deadhead** spent flowers; remove decayed plant parts.
- ☐ **Take 3" to 4" cuttings** of geraniums, begonias, and fuchsias. Root them in damp Perlite in small plastic pots. Put the pots in a shady spot and keep the Perlite moist.
- ☐ **Start moving houseplants indoors.**
- ☐ **Divide and transplant perennials** after they have finished blooming.
- ☐ **Plant fall vegetables** and lettuce (in shade).

August To-Do List

Week 1

Week 2

Week 3

Week 4

August Journal

Manns'
SUPERIOR
MARKET GARDENERS' CATALOGUE
1934
SEEDS
J. MANNS & CO.
FORREST AND HILLEN STS.
BALTIMORE, MD.
Flower Seed Catalogue Mailed on Request

August Journal (cont'd)

DREER'S
AUTUMN
CATALOGUE
1901
BULBS
PLANTS
SEEDS ETC.
HENRY A DREER
714 CHESTNUT ST.

September

What to Do In the Garden

- ☐ **Weed around shrubs** and refresh mulch. Spread a layer of compost before mulching to encourage spring growth.
- ☐ **Side-dress tomatoes and peppers.** Pick green tomatoes before the first frost.
- ☐ **Cut back leggy annuals.**
- ☐ **Plant seeds or transplants** of cool-weather vegetables.
- ☐ **Label and store** leftover seeds for next year.
- ☐ **Move your houseplants indoors** before the first hard frost.
- ☐ **Stake tall-growing autumn flowers,** such as salvia, dahlias, and chrysanthemums.
- ☐ **Spread manure/compost** on your flower beds.
- ☐ **Plant perennials,** spring-flowering bulbs, evergreens, and conifers.

For warmer regions:

- ☐ **Erect shade covers** for vegetables such as tomatoes and peppers.
- ☐ **Last call** to fertilize citrus trees.
- ☐ **Deadhead flowers** of summer-blooming annuals.
- ☐ **Divide perennials,** such as bearded irises and peonies.
- ☐ **Sow seeds of perennials** and set out transplants of petunias, baby's breath, dianthus, snapdragons, yarrow, and geraniums.
- ☐ **Sow seeds or transplants** of herbs, peas, root crops, cool-weather vegetables, and green leafy vegetables.
- ☐ **Plant trees and shrubs.** Water deeply and mulch to the drip line.
- ☐ **Fertilize** dahlias and chrysanthemums. Cut back scraggly and leggy plants.

For colder regions:

- ☐ **If you live in a region** where winter temperatures drop below 20°F for extended periods, lift and store tender bulbs, such as cannas and dahlias, after the first frost.
- ☐ **Divide and transplant** peonies and irises.
- ☐ **Pinch off** tomato flowers and blossoms of pumpkins and winter squash.
- ☐ **Plant cool-weather annuals** and ornamentals, such as pansies and ornamental cabbage.

September To-Do List

Week 1

Week 2

Week 3

Week 4

September Journal

September Journal (cont'd)

October

What to Do In the Garden

- ☐ **Cut back** and divide perennials.
- ☐ **Take cuttings from shrubs and pot them.**
- ☐ **Plant trees, shrubs, and roses,.**
- ☐ **Plant tulips and other spring-flowering bulbs.**
- ☐ **Lift and store** tuberous begonias in a cool **place.**
- ☐ **Wrap hardware cloth** around the base of small fruit trees and roses to protect them from rodents.
- ☐ **Pot up** amaryllis bulbs for indoor blooms during the holidays; grow paperwhites on pebbles in water.
- ☐ **Begin cleaning up** the garden and start a new compost pile.
- ☐ **Bring houseplants indoors.**
- ☐ **Clean and sharpen** garden tools.

For warmer regions:

- ☐ **Plant cool-weather herbs**, such as parsley, cilantro, and dill.
- ☐ **Plant fast-growing c**ool-weather vegetables, such as carrots, radishes, lettuce, and spinach.
- ☐ **Plant spring-flowering bulbs** and perennials.
- ☐ **Plant fruit** and pecan trees. Plant strawberries, blueberries, and grapes.
- ☐ **If frost is predicted** cover plants at night. Add compost to planting beds. Add lime if necessary.

- ☐ **Plant seeds and transplants** of herbs and cool-weather vegetables.
- ☐ **Plant roses,** perennials, and bulbs.
- ☐ **Deadhead** mums and divide clumps of existing bulbs.
- ☐ **Prune fruit trees,** crepe myrtle, hedges, and roses.

For colder regions:

- ☐ **Cut down** dead woody stems on perennials, and cover garden beds with mulch
- ☐ **To protect rose bushes** from winter wind, cut them to 12"-18" above the ground, lightly mulch, and cover them with wood baskets (an old New England trick).
- ☐ **Last call to plant** spring-flowering bulbs.
- ☐ **Lift and divide** summer-blooming bulbs as needed; lift and store gladiolus and tender tubers.
- ☐ **Harvest** or heavily mulch root vegetables.
- ☐ **Plant garli**c and shallots

October To-Do List

Week 1

Week 2

Week 3

Week 4

October Journal

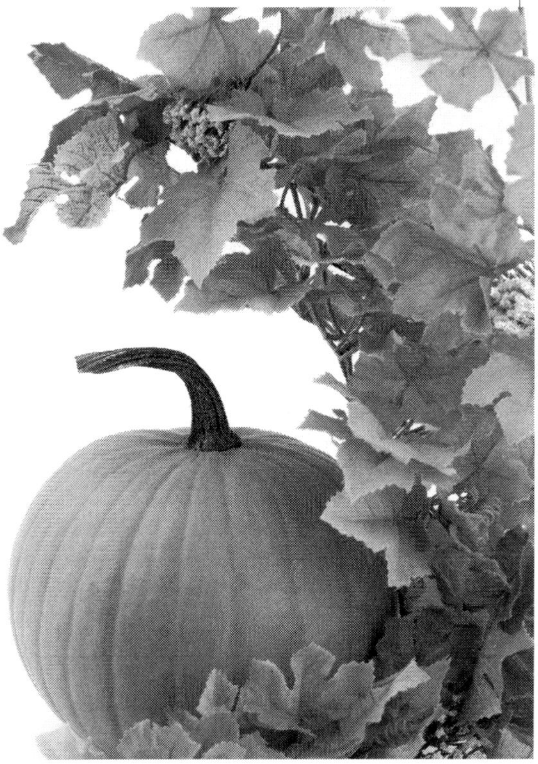

October Journal (cont'd)

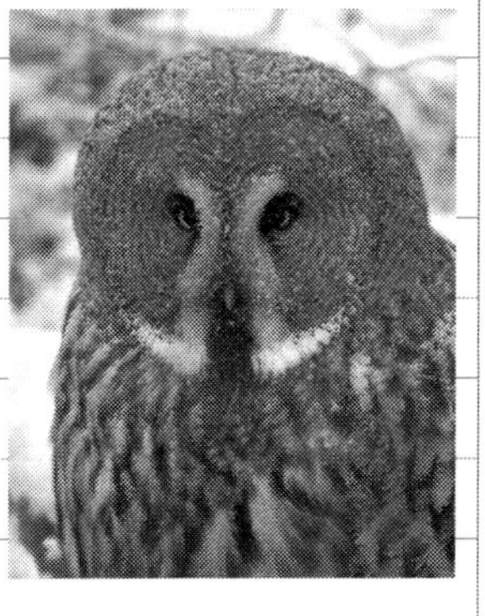

November

What to Do In the Garden

- ☐ **Keep trees and shrubs watered** if rain is scarce. Remove weak and broken limbs.

- ☐ **Dig up tender bulbs** such as cannas, gladiolus, and dahlias. Let them cure, and store them in boxes of peat moss or bark chips in a cool, dry location.

- ☐ **Sow wildflowers.**

- ☐ **Prune** evergreen hedges.

- ☐ **Drain** outdoor watering hoses, roll them up and store in a dry location.

- ☐ **You can plant daffodils** and tulip bulbs if the ground is not frozen.

- ☐ **After the soil is frozen,** cover strawberries with a straw mulch.

- ☐ **If you're getting a live Christmas tree,** dig the hole before the ground is frozen. Keep the soil from the hole where it won't freeze.

- ☐ **Mulch tender plants,** but don't mulch right up to a plant's crown or to the trunks of trees.

- ☐ **Transplant** trees, shrubs, and ornamentals.

- ☐ **Stake** large trees and shrubs to protect them from wind.

- ☐ **Cut the tops off** asparagus plants and add manure to the bed.

For warmer regions:

- ☐ **Sow** sweet peas. Plant evergreens, deciduous trees, spring bulbs, perennials, and annuals.

- ☐ **Clean up** under fruit trees. Destroy fallen and dried-up fruit.

- ☐ **Cover** spinach and lettuce if frost threatens.

- ☐ **Cut back perennials** to a few inches (except spring-bloomers, roses, and chrysanthemums).

- ☐ **Mulch** around shallow-rooted plants after temperatures drop, keeping mulch a few inches away from stems. Fertilize citrus trees with composted manure.

For colder regions:

- ☐ **Cover evergreens** near a road with burlap to protect them from salt spray applied to roads.

- ☐ **Mulch** around tender plants, keeping mulch a few inches away from the base of plants.

- ☐ **After the ground freezes,** cover perennial beds with a thick layer of mulch, shredded leaves, straw, or evergreen branches.

- ☐ **Mulch** around trees, but leave space around the trunks.

- ☐ **Don't prune** boxwood, azaleas, and roses. It would stimulate new growth susceptible to freeze damage.

November To-Do List

Week 1

Week 2

Week 3

Week 4

November Journal

November Journal

December

What to Do In the Garden

- ☐ **Make sure newly planted trees** are staked and supported with guy wire to prevent them from being uprooted by wind and the weight of ice.

- ☐ **Daffodils** can be planted if the ground is not frozen.

- ☐ **Keep straw around vegetables** still in the garden.

- ☐ **Check bulbs,** corms, and tubers you have brought indoors for rot or dessication.

- ☐ **At the end of the month,** cut off Christmas tree branches and lay them over perennials and winter flowers such as pansies.

For warmer regions:

- ☐ **Be prepared to cover tender plants** in case of a sudden drop in temperature. Cover plants with row covers, newspapers, or blankets. If frost is predicted, water plants thoroughly.

- ☐ **Plant** trees and shrubs.

- ☐ **Plant** cool-weather vegetables and annuals.

- ☐ **Plant** spring-flowering bulbs.

- ☐ **Plant** shrubs and bare-root trees.

- ☐ **Prepare planting beds** with compost and manure for spring planting.

- ☐ **Drain** outdoor faucets and slip an insulating **cover over them.**

- ☐ **Prune** damaged wood from fruit or shade trees. Don't prune spring-flowering shrubs.

For colder regions:

- ☐ **Check trees and shrubs** for insect egg masses and for other signs of insect trouble.

- ☐ **Check stored vegetables,** tubers, corms, and bulbs for dessication or rot. Remove any spoiled ones .

- ☐ **On warm days,** trim and mulch perennials.

- ☐ **Wrap trees** to protect them from deer and rabbits.

- ☐ **Plant your live Christmas tree** in the hole you dug last month

- ☐ **Protect** perennial beds with cut Christmas tree limbs.

- ☐ **Start planning** your spring garden. Order seeds for spring vegetables you can start inside next month.

- ☐ **Now is the time** to order seeds for lettuce, peas, onions and other early spring vegetables so that they arrive in January or February for inside planting.

- ☐ **Remember,** you can start your spring seedlings inside the house or in a cold frame.

December To-Do List

Week 1

Week 2

Week 3

Week 4

December Journal

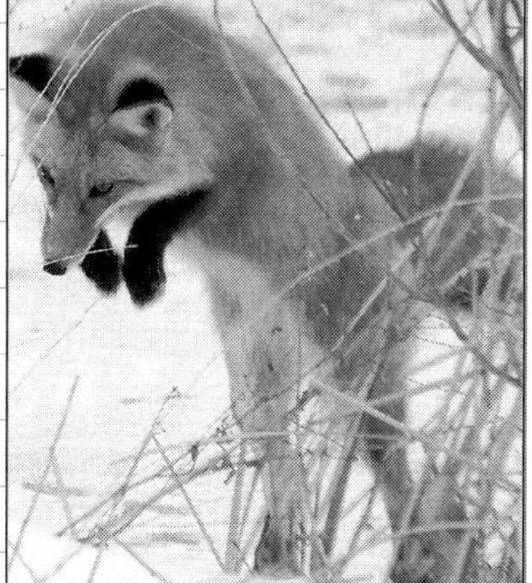

December Journal cont'd

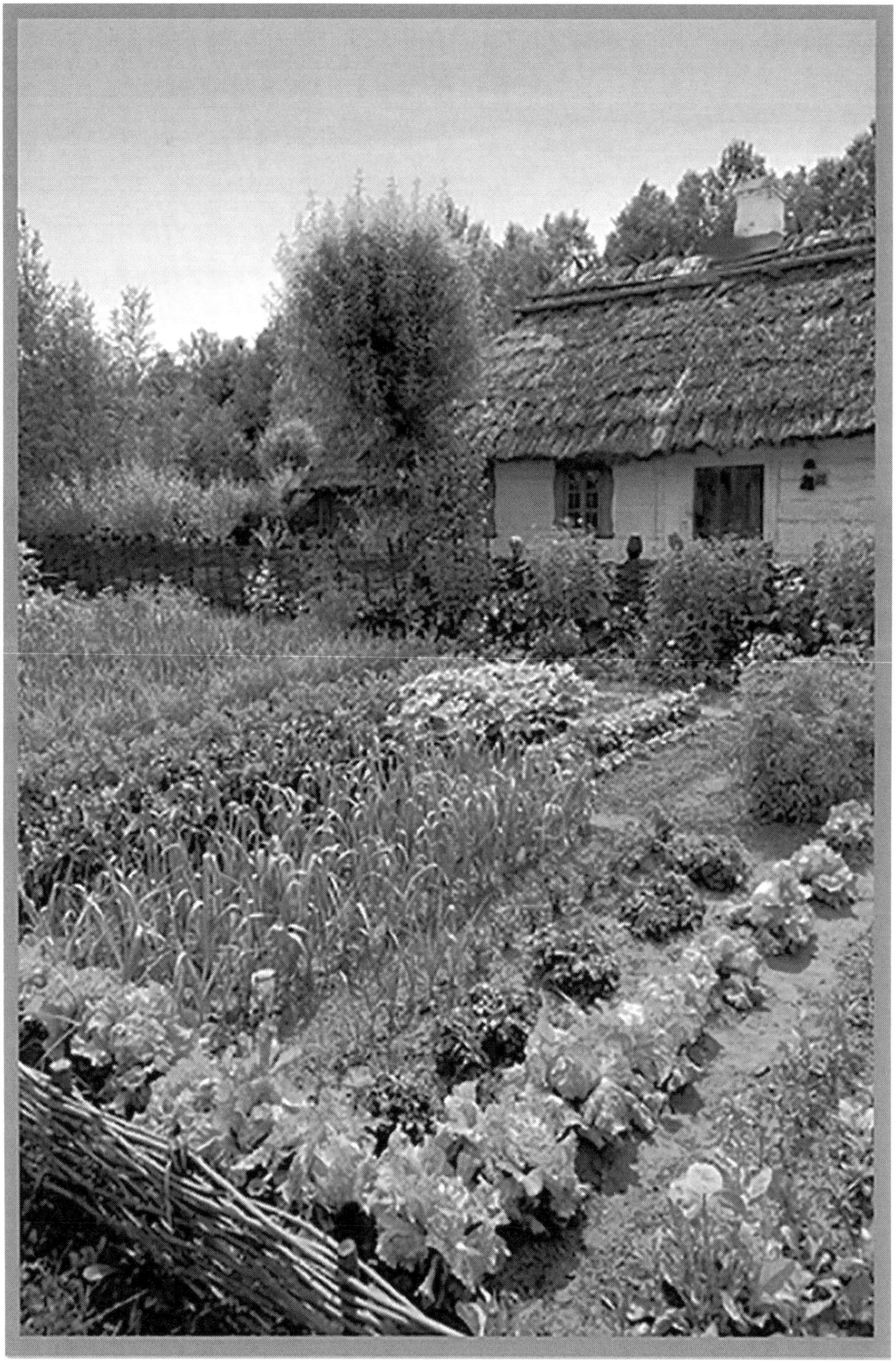

Garden Planner

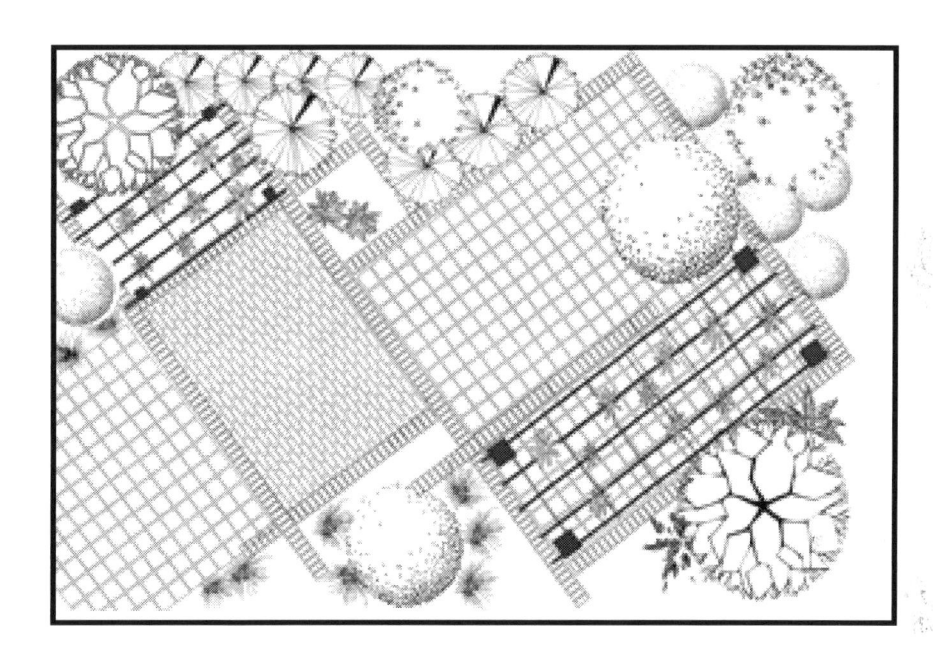

- **GRID PAGES for laying out and planning your garden**

- **SKETCH BOOK and PHOTO ALBUM Pages for sketching, displaying your garden photographs — and more!**

Grid Pages

The grids on the pages that follow are useful in planning the layout of your garden and planting beds. Each block on the grid is a one-half inch square, which could easily represent a square foot of garden space.

If you need more grids or different grid sizes, you can create your own grids or graph paper using a "create table" feature of a word processing program. (Make cells the same size—whatever size you choose.)

Useful Websites

Grids are available to download free on the Internet. Some sites are:

    http://incompetech.com/graphpaper/
    http://www.printablepaper.net/
    http://www.printablepaper.net/preview/1x1
    http://www.vertex42.com/ExcelTemplates/graph-paper.html
    http://donnayoung.org/math/graph-paper.htm
    http://www.activityvillage.co.uk/grid-papers

Free "Plan-a-Garden" Tool/App

Better Homes and Gardens provides a free garden planning tool on their site. They invite you to, "Design the garden of your dreams with our easy drag & drop garden planning tool. " You choose your plants according to type (conifers, perennials, etc.), size, and light requirements; your garden structures (arbors, fences, etc.); and your textures (lawn, old brick, etc.). To get started you may choose from a selection of the most popular garden plans or create your own, using your own photographs of your garden space. "

Try it out! The site also has links to more free garden plans, landscaping basics, and more!

    http://www.bhg.com/app/plan-a-garden/

Sketch Book and Photo Album

Pages for Your Sketches. Photographs, Notes And More!

Handbook of Useful Garden Forms

- **Annual Gardening Calendar**
- **Seeding Schedule**
- **Planting Schedule**
- **Pest Control**
- **Winners!**
- **Losers!**
- **Rainfall Amounts**
- **Wish List**
- **Suppliers, Orders, & Contact Information**
- **Expenses**
- **Plant Profiles**

ANNUAL GARDENiNG CALENDAR

Insert Dates for What You've Done and/or Plan to Do

	Jan.	Feb.	March	April	May	June
SOIL PREPARATION						
PLANTING Indoor: Seed Starters						
Direct Sow: Vegetables						
Direct Sow: Others						
TRANSPLANTING						
IRRIGATION/ WATERING						
FERTILIZING						
PEST CONTROL						
HARVESTING						

July	Aug.	Sept.	Oct.	Nov.	Dec.	NOTES

SEEDING SCHEDULE

DATE	PLANT & VARIETY	SEED SOURCE	AMOUNT SEEDED	SPROUT DATE	TRANSPLANT DATE & LOCATION

SEEDING SCHEDULE cont'd

DATE	PLANT & VARIETY	SEED SOURCE	AMOUNT SEEDED	SPROUT DATE-	TRANSPLANT DATE & LOCATION

PLANTING SCHEDULE

Date	Source of Plant	Seed or Transplant	Date Planted	Planted Where?	Date of Bloom/ Fruit	Notes

PLANTING SCHEDULE cont'd

Date	Source of Plant	Seed or Transplant	Date Planted	Planted Where?	Date of Bloom/ Fruit	Notes

PEST CONTROL

Plant(s)	Pests Observed & Severity of Infestation	Treated How?	Date Treated	Notes

PEST CONTROL cont'd

Plant(s)	Pests Observed & Severity of Infestation	Treated How?	Date Treated	Notes

WINNERS!
Plants and/or plant varieties that worked out well and that you' plant again.

PLANT	NOTES

LOSERS!
Plants and/or plant varieties to never plant again.

PLANT	NOTES

RAINFALL AMOUNTS

	DATES	AMOUNT OF RAINFALL	TOTAL FOR MONTH
Jan.			
Feb.			
March			
April			
May			
June			
July			
Aug.			
Sept.			
Oct.			
Nov.			
Dec,			

WISH LIST

DESCRIPTION	PRICE	NOTES

SUPPLIERS, ORDERS, & CONTACT INFORMATION

Supplier	Contact Information	NOTES

SUPPLIERS, ORDERS, & CONTACT INFORMATION cont'd

Supplier	Contact Information	NOTES

EXPENSES

DATE	DESCRIPTION	SOLD BY	PRICE	HOW PAID	NOTES

EXPENSES cont'd

DATE	DESCRIPTION	SOLD BY	PRICE	HOW PAID	NOTES

PLANT PROFILES

Keep track of the plants in your garden – their characteristics, and what they require in order to thrive. You can find such information on plant tags, seed packets, etc. But there are also two excellent websites with plant databases to supply the information you need. They are:

The National Gardening Association Plants Database: **https://garden.org/plants/**

Learn2Grow Plant Search: **http://www.learn2grow.com/plants**

PLANT	CHARACTERISTICS & REQUIREMENTS	PLANT CARE

PLANT PROFILES cont'd

PLANT	CHARACTERISTICS & REQUIREMENTS	PLANT CARE

PLANT PROFILES cont'd

PLANT	CHARACTERISTICS & REQUIREMENTS	PLANT CARE

PLANT PROFILES cont'd

PLANT	CHARACTERISTICS & REQUIREMENTS	PLANT CARE

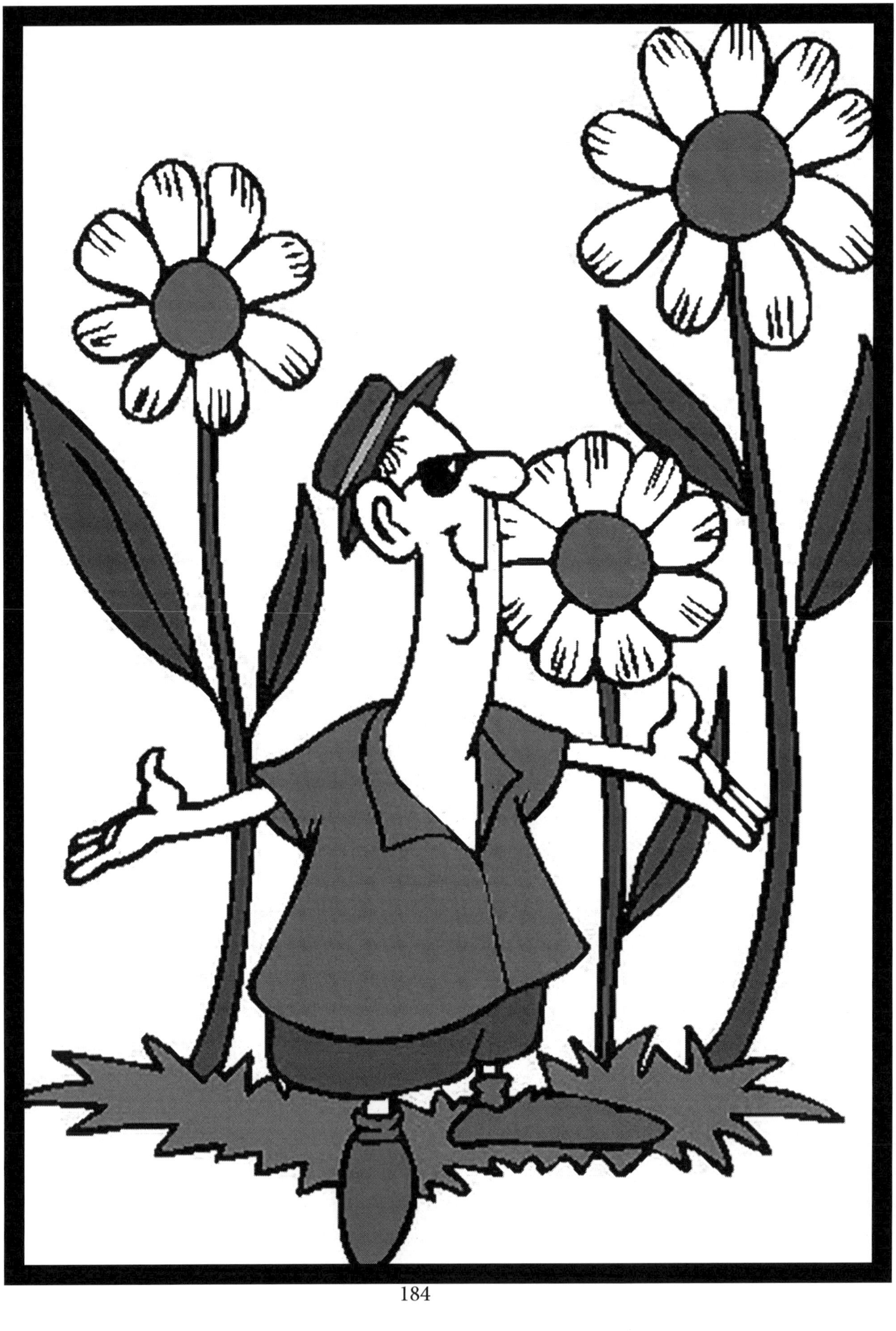

BONUS! HOW TO PUT THIS BOOK IN A 3-RING BINDER

Some gardeners like to keep their gardening information and notes in a 3-ring binder. If you would like to do this, you will find that your *Garden Journal and Planner* was designed to make it easy to put in a binder. It is the same size as 3-hole notebook pages: 8½" x 11".

- Like notebook pages, its format is vertical, not horizontal.
- Inner margins are large to allow for 3-hole punching.
- Pages are numbered, in case they become mixed up when disassembling.
- The binding is glued, making it easy to "unbind."

There are several methods to "unbind" the book and punch holes in its pages. They are described below. All are easy and none of them are expensive. In fact, the first method described does not need to cost a thing

Advantages to Using a 3-Ring Binder

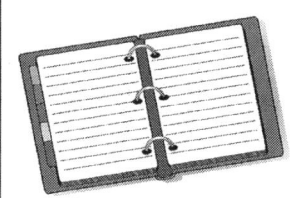

- Additional pages can be added; sections can be rearranged.
- Printed pages and forms can easily be removed and copied.
- Different sections of the book can be put in different binders.

Accessories Available for a 3-Ring Binder

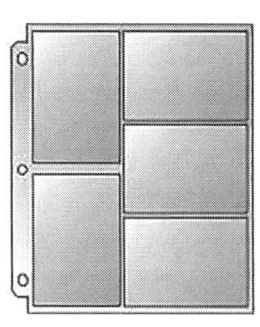

- Divider pages with tabs. Many styles. Some are color-coded.
- Plastic sheet protectors.
- Clear plastic photo-storage pages. These can be used for photos, plant tags, seed packets, etc.
- Hole reinforcements.
- Binders are available with a clear plastic envelope on the front so you can slide in the cover of your choice.
- Some binders have flaps inside the front and back covers to hold loose papers.

HOW TO "UNBIND" AND HOLE-PUNCH THE BOOK

Hair Dryer Method

1. Bend back the front cover and with the dryer on high heat, direct it down between the cover and front page to melt the glue. Do the same thing between the back cover and last page. Apply more heat, if needed, and pull off the cover. Peel the glue residue off the spine.

2. Carefully peel off the pages 2 or 3 at a time, reheating the glue binding as needed. When you are finished, peel off any remaining binding glue.

3. Punch the pages with a 3-hole punch and reassemble them in a loose leaf binder. If you don't have a 3-hole punch, lay a sheet of 3-hole paper over the pages as a template to mark the holes to be punched.

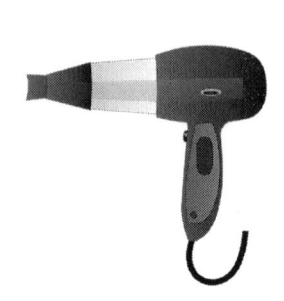

Using Stores That Have Printing Services

Stores such as FedEx-Kinko, Staples, and Office Depot can cut off the binding for you and 3-hole punch the pages. Check your local stores for prices. At the present time, for example, my local office supply store charges $1.99 to cut off the binding and $4.99 to punch holes in the pages. FedEx-Kinko charges $1.49 to cut off the binding and a penny a page to 3-hole punch. But you are welcome to come in and use their 3-hole punch at no charge if you want to do it yourself. In general, FedEx-Kinko stores use a bigger guillotine-type cutter than office supply stores and are better equipped to cut off book bindings, especially for thicker books.

Drill the Page Holes

If you use this method, drill the holes in the book first, before removing the cover and binding.

1. Use a sheet of 3-hole paper as a template. Place it on top of the book's front cover and mark each hole with an X.

2. Put a clamp on the book to keep the pages together while you drill and lay the book face up on a piece of scrap wood for drilling.

3. Drill through each hole with a battery operated or electric drill, using a drill bit the approximate size of a page hole. Use a new sharp drill bit for best results.

4. Remove the book's cover and carefully peel off the pages. Use a hair dryer, as needed, to melt the book's glue binding.

5. Reassemble the book's pages in a 3-ring binder.

Cut Off the Binding

The book can also be "unbound" by cutting off the binding with a utility knife or by using a quilting ruler and rotary cutter. If using the latter, line up the ruler next to the spine and run the rotary cutter along the ruler. Apply some pressure to cut several pages at a time.

SOME USEFUL SITES & BLOGS

American Horticultural Society: ahsgardening .org
National Gardening Society: garden.org
USDA Plants Database plantsusda.gov

Creative Living and Gardening with Bren: brenhaas.com
A Way to Garden: awaytogarden.com
Garden Rant: gardenrant.com
Cold Climate Gardening: coldclimategardening.com
Veggie Gardening Tips: veggiegardeningtips.com
Backyard Gardening Blog: gardeningblog.net
You Grow Girl: The Dirt: yougrowgirl.com/the-dirt-on-soil-2
Your Small Kitchen Garden: smallkitchengarden.net
Garden Design Online: BHG.com

And, if you enjoyed this book, please visit my site,
Gotta Garden: gottagarden.com

BONUS!

FREE BOOK!
Container Gardening

How to Grow Vegetables, Herbs, & Flowers Anywhere

To download the PDF, go to: http://gottagarden.com/?page_id=624

Author's Note

Thanks so much for choosing the *Garden Journal and Planner*. I hope you enjoyed using the book and that it helped make your gardening year both easier and more fun.

If so, I'd like to ask you for a favor. Would you please leave a review on Amazon.com giving your opinion about the helpfulness of the book. I would really appreciate it, and reviews are very useful to those trying to make a decision about which book would best meet their needs.

To leave a review, just go to the book's page on Amazon.com and scroll down to the section "Customer Reviews." At the bottom of that section, click on the box *"Write a customer review."* I would love to have your feedback on the book.

Happy gardening!

Michelle Marsh

www.GottaGarden.com
@mygardenbook
gardenjournal129@gmail.com

Also by Michelle Marsh...

Grow a beautiful, NO-COST indoor garden from kitchen scraps!

Veggies, Fruit, Herbs, Houseplants, Vines...

from scraps you would ordinarily toss in the garbage!

It's Easy! It's Fun!

A great family project!

Made in the USA
Lexington, KY
19 November 2017